THE HOLY SPIRIT

by
Andrew Wommack

Unless otherwise indicated, all Scripture quotations are taken from the *King James Version* of the Bible.

The Holy Spirit
ISBN 1-59548-053-6
Copyright © 2005 by Andrew Wommack Ministries, Inc.
850 Elkton Dr.
Colorado Springs, CO 80907

Published by Andrew Wommack Ministries, Inc.

TABLE
OF
CONTENTS

Introduction

Millions of Christians today have received God's power into their lives through the separate, distinct experience called "the baptism in the Holy Spirit." Wherever you go in the world—Africa, Asia, Europe, North and South America, Australia—these believers are aggressively and effectively advancing the kingdom of God!

I grew up being told that God's miraculous power had ceased on earth with the passing of the early Church. This led me to believe that I had received all of the Holy Spirit I could get at salvation. After being saved for many years, I became frustrated with my powerless, defeated Christian life. In desperation, I sought the Lord with all my heart and stumbled into the baptism in the Holy Spirit. This powerful encounter with God revolutionized my entire life!

Today, over 35 years later, my relationship with the Lord is deeper and stronger than ever before. I regularly see miracles of every kind, and my teaching ministry literally reaches around the world. None of this would have been possible apart from the supernatural power of the Holy Spirit!

Whether you are newly born again or have been saved for many years, God's Word clearly reveals that the baptism in the Holy Spirit is necessary, standard equipment for living a fruitful and fulfilled Christian life. The Lord Himself commanded: **"Receive ye the Holy Ghost"** (John 20:22). I encourage you to do so today!

Chapter *1*

Empowered Lives

I was born again at eight years old. Our pastor had preached a message on hell in church that morning. Even though I hadn't done many terrible things in my young life, I recognized that I had sinned and fallen short of the glory of God. I knew "hell" was a place where people who didn't accept Jesus as their Lord and Savior went. This concerned me, so I asked my father about it. He explained God's holiness and how sin separated me from Him. He also told me how God's justice demanded that I go to hell. Then Dad made it clear that Jesus came to forgive my sin and suffer the punishment in my place. I remember praying with my father to receive the Lord right there in my bedroom. Immediately, I felt an inner release as peace flooded my heart.

The next day at school, my friends noticed the change in me before I'd told anyone of my conversion. "What's different with you?" they asked. When I answered that I'd been born again, they immediately started making fun of me for being a Christian. Although these classmates recognized an initial difference at my conversion, subsequent evidence for my faith in Christ was meager at best.

My closest friend from grade school never knew I was a Christian until he saw me recently on television. He'd just gone through an extremely difficult time in life and had reached out to receive the Lord from the absolute end of his rope. While visiting with each other for the first time in over thirty years, he was totally shocked to discover that I'd been a Christian the whole time we were friends together growing up!

My faith simply didn't affect anyone else's life! I prayed six months straight for my father to be healed, but nothing happened. He died when I was twelve. Although I easily overcame temptations others yielded to, the tangible demonstrations of God's power described of believers in the Bible were noticeably absent from my life. Basically, Christianity to me was just the doctrines and beliefs I held inside.

Then on March 23, 1968, I received the baptism in the Holy Spirit! Something within me exploded, and my understanding of God immediately shot through the roof. It took many years of renewing my mind before I was able to explain to others the things I instantly knew in my spirit. In fact, my mother thought I'd lost my mind because of the sudden, radical, outward transformation of my soul, my thinking, and my actions. My intense, new zeal for God, coupled at the time with a lack of wisdom, even got me kicked out of a few churches. I'd become a fanatic overnight!

You never would've heard of me if I hadn't been baptized in the Holy Spirit! I would have maintained my nominal salvation, surviving until heaven and making practically no eternal impact here on earth. This prior lack of victory and outward manifestation of God's power isn't unique only to me. I've read many, many testimonies of people who experienced the same thing—even in the Bible!

Like a Dove

Jesus Himself did not manifest the power of God until He had been baptized in the Holy Spirit. Angels pronounced Him Lord at His birth, but nothing that typified Christ's ministry—preaching, healing, casting out demons—occurred before the Holy Spirit descended upon Him like a dove. **"And Jesus, when he was baptized, went up straightway out of the water: and, lo, the heavens were opened unto him, and he saw the Spirit of God descending like a dove, and lighting upon him: And lo a voice from heaven, saying, This is my beloved Son, in whom I am well pleased"** (Matt. 3:16-17). The baptism in the Holy Spirit served as the turning point from natural to supernatural in Christ's life.

Jesus immediately began His ministry after being anointed with the Holy Spirit. The Spirit led Him into the wilderness to confront the devil (Luke 4:1-13). He emerged victorious and boldly declared in the synagogue of His own hometown, **"The Spirit of the Lord is upon me, because he hath anointed me to preach the gospel to the poor; he hath sent me to heal the brokenhearted, to preach deliverance to the captives, and recovering of sight to the blind, to set at liberty them that are bruised, To preach the acceptable year of the Lord"** (Luke 4:18-19). From this point forward, Jesus did what He was anointed to do!

Many times, the Lord admitted His total dependence upon the Father and the Spirit. He did His Father's will as the power of the Holy Spirit flowed in and through Him. Father, Son, and Holy Spirit always worked together in complete cooperation. As a part of this interdependent, triune Godhead, Jesus would not and could not do any miracles until the Holy Spirit had come upon Him.

God never does anything independent of His Spirit. Therefore, welcoming the Holy Spirit into your life is absolutely essential for you to experience the victory and abundance God has provided. If the sinless Son of God had to be baptized in the Holy Spirit before beginning His ministry, how can anyone presume to be an effective Christian without it?

Ruckus in the Temple

The disciples were spineless wimps before receiving the baptism in the Holy Spirit. These men had followed Jesus for three and a half years, observing His miracles, hearing His teaching, and experiencing everyday life with Him. They exhibited weakness, immaturity, carnal-mindedness, and strife. Upon Jesus' arrest, all their promises to stay with Him—to death if need be—went right out the window, as they forsook Him and fled for their lives in terror!

Peter denied Jesus three different times just hours after pledging his "undying allegiance." His natural strength wilted before a damsel, the high priest's maid, and certain others as they each successively asked, "Aren't you one of Jesus' disciples?" Swearing and taking oaths, he answered, "No, I don't even know the Man!" Peter wept bitterly when he realized what he'd done. He hadn't wanted to deny Christ but was powerless not to in his own human strength (Matt. 26:69-75).

Then Peter and the other disciples were baptized in the Holy Spirit. **"And when the day of Pentecost was fully come, they were all with one accord in one place. And suddenly there came a sound from heaven as of a rushing mighty wind...And they were all filled with the Holy Ghost"** (Acts 2:1-2, 4). They instantly transformed into powerful witnesses and testified of Jesus with great boldness. Three thousand were saved and water baptized that first day alone (Acts 2:41)!

5

Shortly thereafter, Peter and John healed a lame man in front of the temple and caused such a ruckus preaching the Gospel that the religious leaders threw them in jail (Acts 3-4:3). Thousands more believed their message, so the leaders interrogated Peter and John to find out what was going on. **"And it came to pass on the morrow, that their rulers, and elders, and scribes, And Annas the high priest, and Caiaphas, and John, and Alexander, and as many as were of the kindred of the high priest, were gathered together at Jerusalem. And when they had set them in the midst, they asked, By what power, or by what name, have ye done this"** (Acts 4:5-7).

Peter boldly confronted the same men who had crucified Jesus! **"Then Peter, filled with the Holy Ghost, said unto them, Ye rulers of the people, and elders of Israel, If we this day be examined of the good deed done to the impotent man, by what means he is made whole; Be it known unto you all, and to all the people of Israel, that by the name of Jesus Christ of Nazareth, whom ye crucified, whom God raised from the dead, even by him doth this man stand here before you whole. This is the stone which was set at nought of you builders, which is become the head of the corner. Neither is there salvation in any other: for there is none other name under heaven given among men, whereby we must be saved"** (Acts 4:8-12). Peter publicly declared to the entire Jewish leadership that belief in the God of Abraham alone was insufficient for salvation. He clearly told them to believe on the name of Jesus Christ, whom they themselves had killed, or face eternal damnation. Peter left them no avenue of escape: Either accept Jesus or reject Him!

The same men from whom the disciples had once fled in terror were now backing down in the face of their inspired boldness: **"Now when they saw the boldness of Peter and John, and perceived that they were unlearned and ignorant men, they marvelled; and they took knowledge of them, that they had been with Jesus. And beholding the man which was healed standing with them, they could say nothing against it"** (Acts 4:13-14). The miracle worked by the disciples completely silenced the religious leaders' opposition. What a difference the baptism in the Holy Spirit makes!

Clear Instructions

Our Lord's last words to His followers before ascending were clear instructions regarding the Holy Spirit. If your work on earth was done and you were leaving to return to your Father in heaven and were about to turn your entire kingdom over to a small group of people, your last words to them would be very important.

Jesus commanded His disciples not to do anything until they had been baptized in the Holy Spirit. **"And, being assembled together with them, commanded them that they should not depart from Jerusalem, but wait for the promise of the Father, which, saith**

he, ye have heard of me. For John truly baptized with water; but ye shall be baptized with the Holy Ghost not many days hence...But ye shall receive power, after that the Holy Ghost is come upon you: and ye shall be witnesses unto me both in Jerusalem, and in all Judea, and in Samaria, and unto the uttermost part of the earth. And when he had spoken these things, while they beheld, he was taken up; and a cloud received him out of their sight" (Acts 1:4-5, 8-9).

Think about how difficult this must have been for the disciples! Jesus had preached God's Word and demonstrated His power on earth like no one ever before. Due to this, the religious leaders had Him killed and buried. To their natural minds, it appeared as if Jesus had been just another man. Yet three days later, He arose from the dead exactly as He prophesied, validating everything He had said. As if that wasn't enough, Jesus spent forty more days on earth after His resurrection teaching His followers before they personally watched Him ascend to His Father in heaven. These disciples had incredibly good news—news worth shouting from the rooftops—but Jesus commanded them to sit on it temporarily! Why? They needed the baptism in the Holy Spirit!

It's absolutely wonderful to be born again and forgiven of your sins, but you won't be an effective witness until you have the fullness of the Holy Spirit. When He comes, you'll be able to live in victory and testify in power. The Holy Spirit enables you to more fully experience your salvation and to effectively share with others the awesome things God has done for you!

Many Christians sincerely love God, but serve Him in their own power, because they haven't been baptized in His Spirit. This results in deadness. **"Who also hath made us able ministers of the new testament; not of the letter, but of the spirit: for the letter killeth, but the spirit giveth life"** (2 Cor. 3:6). When believers try to minister out of their own carnal knowledge and ability—even when they say and do the right thing—it just doesn't carry any spiritual weight. So much of the deadness in the church today stems from believers attempting to minister without Holy Spirit empowerment.

Jesus Christ Himself testifies and ministers His life through Holy Spirit-empowered witnesses. Your Spirit-energized words and deeds will carry weight to positively impact other people's lives for the kingdom of God. The Holy Spirit is the One who will help you experience the promised life of victory and abundance. If both Jesus and the early believers needed to be baptized in the Holy Spirit in order to live powerful Christian lives, so do you and I today!

Chapter 2

Baptized in the Holy Spirit

If you believe the Word of God, you cannot dispute the existence of a "baptism in the Holy Spirit." Speaking of Jesus, John the Baptist said, **"I indeed baptize you with water unto repentance: but he that cometh after me is mightier than I, whose shoes I am not worthy to bear: he shall baptize you with the Holy Ghost, and with fire"** (Matt. 3:11). Christ was baptized in the Holy Spirit (Matt. 3:16, Mark 1:10, and Luke 3:22). The early apostles, including Paul, were baptized in the Holy Spirit (Acts 2:1-4, 9:17-18). Whenever people were born again in the book of Acts, they also received the baptism in the Holy Spirit soon thereafter.

Many Christians claim that the baptism in the Holy Spirit comes automatically at salvation. **"No man can come to me, except the Father which hath sent me draw him: and I will raise him up at the last day"** (John 6:44). They recognize the Spirit's work in drawing people to God and assume that you get all of the Holy Spirit you can the moment you're born again. Although it's true you have the Holy Spirit once you're saved, that doesn't mean you've been baptized in Him!

Rivers of Living Water

It's one thing to have the Holy Spirit and quite another for the Holy Spirit to have you! There are major differences between having the Holy Spirit present in your life and having the Holy Spirit in control of your life. Spiritually speaking, it's night and day.

Jesus told His disciples, **"And I will pray the Father, and he shall give you another Comforter, that he may abide with you for ever; Even the Spirit of truth; whom the world cannot receive, because it seeth him not, neither knoweth him: but ye know him; for he dwelleth with you, and shall be in you"** (John 14:16-17).

Prior to Jesus' resurrection, the Holy Spirit couldn't be received the way we are discussing. He was present *with* the disciples and worked through them (as evidenced by the miracles they did), but He wasn't *in* them.

This was because the fullness of the Holy Spirit couldn't be received until after Christ had ascended back to heaven in glory.

When the Holy Spirit is in you, rivers of life flow out from your innermost being. **"Jesus stood and cried, saying, If any man thirst, let him come unto me, and drink. He that believeth on me, as the scripture hath said, out of his belly shall flow rivers of living water. (But this spake he of the Spirit, which they that believe on him should receive: for the Holy Ghost was not yet given; because that Jesus was not yet glorified.)"** (John 7:37-39). Not just a trickle or a cupful, not even a well you have to pump, but *rivers* of living water will bubble out from within you like an artesian spring!

Jesus promised His disciples that the Holy Spirit who had been with them would one day be in them. That day arrived shortly after His ascension. **"And when the day of Pentecost was fully come, they were all with one accord in one place. And suddenly there came a sound from heaven as of a rushing mighty wind, and it filled all the house where they were sitting. And there appeared unto them cloven tongues like as of fire, and it sat upon each of them. And they were all filled with the Holy Ghost, and began to speak with other tongues, as the Spirit gave them utterance"** (Acts 2:1-4).

The Power Source

Those who don't believe that the baptism in the Holy Spirit is a second, separate experience from salvation erroneously teach that God's miraculous power ceased with the passing of the first apostles. They don't believe in the gifts of the Spirit, speaking in tongues, or casting out demons—nor living in victory over sickness, disease, and poverty. They believe that if you see any of these miracles occurring today that God Himself did in the Bible, it's the work of the devil. Something's wrong with this theology!

The Holy Spirit is the power Source! Reject Him, and you won't see miracles, healings, demons cast out, or speaking in tongues. Accept Him by receiving the baptism in the Holy Spirit, and you open yourself to God's supernatural power working in all these wonderful ways—but you must receive the Source in order to have His power!

A Separate Experience

The Bible makes it clear that the baptism in the Holy Spirit is a separate experience from salvation. The only way you can miss this is if you have some kind of religious prejudice against it. In Acts 8, Philip went to Samaria and preached Christ. Seeing the miracles he did, many believed and were water baptized (Acts 8:5-12). When the church in Jerusalem heard what had happened, they sent Peter and John to check it out. They arrived, saw those who had been saved, and then laid hands on them to receive the baptism in the Holy Spirit (Acts 8:14-17).

Some people assume, "You aren't really saved until you're baptized in the Holy Spirit!" Acts 8 soundly refutes this. The Samaritans had received God's Word, were born again, and had been water baptized. If they had died before being baptized in the Holy Spirit, they would've been ushered into the very presence of the Lord Himself. Salvation saves and the baptism in the Holy Spirit empowers!

Certain disciples at Ephesus also demonstrate this truth. **"And it came to pass, that, while Apollos was at Corinth, Paul having passed through the upper coasts came to Ephesus: and finding certain disciples, He said unto them, Have ye received the Holy Ghost since ye believed? And they said unto him, We have not so much as heard whether there be any Holy Ghost"** (Acts 19:1-2).

Apollos had been zealously preaching Jesus wherever he went (Acts 18:24-25). However, he had left the company of the disciples before Christ resurrected and told them about the baptism in the Holy Spirit. Aquila and Priscilla had to take him aside and explain the way of God to him more accurately (Acts 18:26). Before this, Apollos had already made some converts in Ephesus, whom Paul found some time later. When he asked "Have you received the Holy Spirit," they answered, **"We have not so much as heard whether there be any Holy Ghost"** (Acts 19:2). Sounds like many Christians today!

I was raised in church, but no one ever told me I could be supernaturally empowered by the Holy Spirit. I didn't know He wanted to come and work miracles through me. Our church didn't believe in that. We were saved but stuck! Besides winning others to the Lord and singing "when we all get to heaven," there just wasn't anything else to look forward to in our Christian lives. I was ignorant of the fact that God had provided for me to live a victorious, abundant life here on earth!

Apollos' converts believed in Jesus, but didn't know that the Holy Spirit had been sent to anoint them as their Lord had been anointed. Paul picked up where Apollos left off and shared with these Ephesian believers how they could receive God's power into their lives. **"And when Paul had laid his hands upon them, the Holy Ghost came on them; and they spake with tongues, and prophesied"** (Acts 19:6).

Impact Your World!

Millions of people alive today can testify to this separate, distinct work of the Holy Spirit in their lives after salvation. Although many born-again Christians in Western countries deny this experience, the majority of believers in the rest of the world have welcomed the baptism in the Holy Spirit!

Africa, Asia, and South America have experienced some of the greatest outpourings we've seen in recent times. Miracles regularly happen and churches sometimes number into the tens, even hundreds of thousands. The vast majority of believers involved in these outpourings have received the baptism in the Holy Spirit with speaking in tongues.

Across the body of Christ worldwide, the parts that are experiencing the most growth are those who believe in the baptism in the Holy Spirit. Most traditional, denominational churches that fight against this gift have either stagnated or are suffering serious decline. Spirit-baptized believers are progressing in the Christian life, doing most of the effective evangelism and making the biggest impact for the advancing kingdom of God.

Do you want to be where God's power is moving? Are you hungry to experience excitement and life? Do you long to join the winning side? You'll find all this and more among believers who have been baptized in the Holy Spirit!

Chapter 3

The Full Package

Jesus often referred to the Holy Spirit as "the Comforter." He'll function in your life many different ways:

The Holy Spirit will abide with you forever. **"And I will pray the Father, and he shall give you another Comforter, that he may abide with you for ever"** (John 14:16). Wherever you go, whatever you do, God Himself will be with you!

The Holy Spirit will comfort you through challenges and difficulties. **"Who comforteth us in all our tribulation, that we may be able to comfort them which are in any trouble, by the comfort wherewith we ourselves are comforted of God"** (2 Cor. 1:4). He'll also enable you to minister God's comfort to others.

The Holy Spirit will be your Teacher. **"But the Comforter, which is the Holy Ghost, whom the Father will send in my name, he shall teach you all things, and bring all things to your remembrance, whatsoever I have said unto you"** (John 14:26). He'll also remind you of everything the Lord has said.

The Spirit of truth will testify to you of Jesus. **"But when the Comforter is come, whom I will send unto you from the Father, even the Spirit of truth, which proceedeth from the Father, he shall testify of me: And ye also shall bear witness, because ye have been with me from the beginning"** (John 15:26-27). He'll also help you bear witness of Jesus to others.

"It's Better That I Go!"

It's to your advantage that Jesus is in heaven and the Holy Spirit is on earth. **"Nevertheless I tell you the truth; It is expedient for you that I go away: for if I go not away, the Comforter will not come unto you; but if I depart, I will send him unto you"** (John 16:7). Jesus could only be in one place at a time when He walked the earth as a man. Now, through His Spirit, He can be with every believer all the time!

The Holy Spirit will convict and convince. **"And when he is come, he will reprove the world of sin, and of righteousness, and of judgment: Of sin, because they believe not on me; Of righteousness, be-**

cause I go to my Father, and ye see me no more; Of judgment, because the prince of this world is judged" (John 16:8-11). He convicts you of not trusting Jesus. He convinces you that you're righteous in Christ, and the devil, who constantly hurls condemnation and lies at you, is judged.

The Holy Spirit will guide you into all truth. "I have yet many things to say unto you, but ye cannot bear them now. Howbeit when he, the Spirit of truth, is come, he will guide you into all truth: for he shall not speak of himself; but whatsoever he shall hear, that shall he speak: and he will shew you things to come" (John 16:12-13). The Spirit of truth will progressively share Jesus' words with you as you're mature enough to handle them. He'll even reveal things yet to come!

The Holy Spirit will glorify Jesus. "He shall glorify me: for he shall receive of mine, and shall shew it unto you" (John 16:14). He'll receive things from the Lord and show them to you!

God's power will flood into you as you're baptized in Him! "But ye shall receive power, after that the Holy Ghost is come upon you: and ye shall be witnesses unto me both in Jerusalem, and in all Judaea, and in Samaria, and unto the uttermost part of the earth" (Acts 1:8). Wherever you go, you'll be an effective witness!

Essential, Not Optional!

In light of all these awesome benefits, I urge you to accept the fact that the baptism in the Holy Spirit is not merely optional but essential. Receive His power so you can fully experience the Comforter!

The baptism in the Holy Spirit makes God's power available to you. Although you're not automatically transformed into a victorious Christian, you'll experience increasing victory as you draw out His power by faith. This is why some people who have received the baptism in the Holy Spirit don't exhibit more victory in their lives. God's power is available to them, but they haven't drawn it out. Those who reject the baptism in the Holy Spirit deny themselves access to His power. You must have received the Source in order to access His power!

Some Christians may have been baptized in the Holy Spirit without realizing it. They are wonderful people who don't speak in tongues or believe in a distinct experience with the Holy Spirit, yet they clearly exhibit all of the other characteristics of someone who has received the baptism. Often, with many of them, there was a time in their lives when they came to the end of themselves. They cried out to the Lord for help, asking for more of Him. After yielding, they had a miraculous encounter with God. Now whether they're aware of what they received or not, if the encounter actually included being baptized in the Holy Spirit, they can now speak in tongues anytime they want just by exercising their faith to do so.

God intends for you to have His full package! Some theologians from the 1800s and early 1900s taught about a second, separate experience with the Lord but didn't teach on speaking in tongues. They believed there had to be an enduing of power from on high but failed to embrace the accompanying miracles. Why receive only part of God's gift? Why not receive it all? Your loving heavenly Father cared enough to give you the baptism in the Holy Spirit. Honor Him by receiving the full package!

Chapter 4

Receive Him Today

God wants you baptized in the Holy Spirit! His longing to fill, control, and empower you far surpasses your desire to be filled, controlled, and empowered. In fact, the Holy Spirit has been eagerly waiting for you to open your heart and invite Him in. If you're ready to ask in faith, why not receive Him today?

Some groups erroneously teach that you must "travail" and wait on God to receive this experience. They believe God will baptize you whenever He wants to, and you have no control over it. This idea is based upon a misinterpretation of Acts 1:4-5, **"And, being assembled together with them, commanded them that they should not depart from Jerusalem, but wait for the**

promise of the Father, which, saith he, ye have heard of me. For John truly baptized with water; but ye shall be baptized with the Holy Ghost not many days hence."

Jesus commanded the disciples to wait for the baptism because the Holy Spirit had not yet been poured out upon the earth. **"And when the day of Pentecost was fully come, they were all with one accord in one place...And they were all filled with the Holy Ghost"** (Acts 2:1, 4). Pentecost was God's appointed time to pour out the Holy Spirit. Since He's already been given, there's now no need to wait!

While seeking the baptism in the Holy Spirit, I was told I had to cleanse myself before I could receive. As instructed, I wrote out every sin I could think of on a couple of sheets of paper in my misguided effort to get "clean enough." Religious logic had deceived me into thinking "A jar full of rocks must be emptied before being filled with water" and "the Holy Spirit won't fill a dirty vessel!" Hogwash!

The baptism in the Holy Spirit is a *gift*, not something you can earn by travail or holiness (Luke 11:13). If you could rid yourself of all the sin in your life and be perfect before receiving the Holy Spirit, you wouldn't need Him! He's the One who will give you the power to be set free from lusts, habits, addictions, and desires. You can be delivered from anything when you receive and draw on the power of the Holy Spirit!

Wholehearted Desire

You need to desire the baptism in the Holy Spirit wholeheartedly. If you are persuaded and hungry, receiving can be as simple as praying a prayer. However, some people have been led to do so before they were really ready. Occasionally, someone needs a period of time to grow in their hunger and desire to receive. Where are you today? Are you persuaded and hungry for the baptism? Do you wholeheartedly desire to invite the Holy Spirit into your life?

Personally, I was desperate for the baptism in the Holy Spirit. I thought I had to pursue God and then wait for it. This misunderstanding only fed my growing hunger to receive. Then, when the baptism came, it was spectacular! Since this was something I'd longed for and sought after, I didn't just forget about it after speaking in tongues once or twice. Over the years, I've cherished this awesome gift from God. Without His power, I wouldn't be living in the victory and abundance I enjoy today—for which I'm eternally grateful!

Are you ready to commit yourself to the Holy Spirit without reservation? Are you hungry to receive God's power into your life? Perhaps you've even recited a prayer for this before but weren't really ready yet. However, after learning these truths—how you'll receive power, that this was something even Jesus had to have, that it totally transformed the apostles—you're ready to receive the baptism in the Holy Spirit now.

Ask, Believe, and Receive!

God wants you filled, but you must reach out in faith to take it! **"For every one that asketh receiveth; and he that seeketh findeth; and to him that knocketh it shall be opened. If a son shall ask bread of any of you that is a father, will he give him a stone? or if he ask a fish, will he for a fish give him a serpent? Or if he shall ask an egg, will he offer him a scorpion? If ye then, being evil, know how to give good gifts unto your children: how much more shall your heavenly Father give the Holy Spirit to them that ask him"** (Luke 11:10-13). How much more will your heavenly Father give the Holy Spirit to you! Ask, believe, and receive!

If you're ready, pray out loud the following prayer from your heart:

Father, I surrender to You completely. I recognize my need for Your power to live the Christian life. I'm hungry for You! Please baptize me in Your Holy Spirit!

By faith, I receive now the baptism in the Holy Spirit. I take it! It's mine in Jesus' name!

Father, thank You for giving me the Holy Spirit! Holy Spirit, thank You for coming. You are welcome in my life!

Continue to praise and thank the Lord for this wonderful gift. Take a few moments to enjoy His presence, and tell Him how much you love Him.

Some people have dramatic experiences receiving the Holy Spirit, and others are genuinely baptized without feeling a thing. One's not better than the other, as long as you received! Don't let outward manifestations, or a lack thereof, enable the devil to talk you out of this gift from God (Matt. 13:19).

If you believed in your heart when you prayed that you received, then God's Word promises that you did. **"Therefore I say unto you, What things soever ye desire, when ye pray, believe that ye receive them, and ye shall have them"** (Mark 11:24). God always honors His Word. Believe it! As you stepped out in faith to obey the direct command of Jesus (John 20:22), you received the baptism in the Holy Spirit.

Congratulations—you've been filled with God's supernatural power! As you learn to tap into this power, your life will never be the same. For the rest of this book, I'm going to share about an important way you can draw His power out.

Chapter 5

Speaking in Tongues

God's Word reveals that speaking in tongues is one of the first manifestations to occur when you receive the baptism in the Holy Spirit.

Jesus' disciples spoke in tongues immediately after receiving the Holy Spirit. **"And when the day of Pentecost was fully come, they were all with one accord in one place. And suddenly there came a sound from heaven as of a rushing mighty wind, and it filled all the house where they were sitting. And there appeared unto them cloven tongues like as of fire, and it sat upon each of them. And they were all filled with the Holy Ghost, and began to speak with other tongues, as the Spirit gave them utterance"** (Acts 2:1-4).

As Peter preached the Gospel to the entire household of Cornelius, they received both salvation and the baptism in the Holy Spirit. **"While Peter yet spake these words, the Holy Ghost fell on all them which heard the word. And they of the circumcision which believed were astonished, as many as came with Peter, because that on the Gentiles also was poured out the gift of the Holy Ghost. For they heard them speak with tongues, and magnify God"** (Acts 10:44-46). Speaking in tongues served as outward evidence that these brand-new believers had truly received the Holy Spirit.

Peter used this fact to prove to the rest of the Jewish believers (who weren't there in person) that these Gentiles had indeed been born again. **"And as I began to speak, the Holy Ghost fell on them, as on us at the beginning. Then remembered I the word of the Lord, how that he said, John indeed baptized with water; but ye shall be baptized with the Holy Ghost. Forasmuch then as God gave them the like gift as he did unto us, who believed on the Lord Jesus Christ; what was I, that I could withstand God? When they heard these things, they held their peace, and glorified God, saying, Then hath God also to the Gentiles granted repentance unto life"** (Acts 11:15-18).

Paul ministered the baptism in the Holy Spirit to Apollos' converts to Christ in Ephesus. **"And when Paul had laid his hands upon them, the Holy Ghost came on them; and they spake with tongues, and proph-**

esied" (Acts 19:6). Speaking in tongues comes with the baptism in the Holy Spirit!

Every Spirit-Baptized Believer

Philip went down to Samaria and evangelized. Many people believed on Jesus when they heard his message and saw the miracles that he did (Acts 8:5-8). Later, Peter and John came to minister the baptism in the Holy Spirit (Acts 8:14-17). As the Samaritans began to receive, one of the new converts, who had been a professional sorcerer, saw them speaking in tongues and lusted for this power selfishly. Peter and John rebuked him for trying to buy God's gift (Acts 8:18-24).

Those who argue against speaking in tongues as initial evidence for the baptism in the Holy Spirit try to use Acts 8 to support their point. However, even though these scriptures don't directly say that the people of Samaria spoke in tongues, there's still plenty of evidence to imply it. Speaking in tongues is present every other time the Holy Spirit was poured out in the book of Acts. Also, this recently converted sorcerer *saw something* when the baptism was ministered that caused him to offer the apostles money in exchange for the supernatural ability to impart the Holy Spirit (verse 18). In order to maintain biblical consistency, this visible demonstration of power must have been speaking in tongues.

Speaking in tongues is an immediate audible manifestation of the Holy Spirit available to every Spirit-baptized believer. It's something you can do to help prove that you've received Him. However, tongues won't automatically force their way up out of your mouth just because you've been baptized. The Holy Spirit will never make you do something against your will. Therefore, you must choose to speak in tongues.

Darkness to Daylight

Personally, I stumbled into the baptism in the Holy Spirit. I had been seeking the Lord with all of my heart and crying out for Him to fill me with His power. On March 23, 1968, He dramatically answered my prayer by baptizing me in the Holy Spirit. At the time, I had no idea what this was because I'd never been taught about it. All I knew was that my intimate encounter with God had left me supernaturally empowered.

Revelation knowledge immediately began to flow. Before receiving the baptism in the Holy Spirit, I always had to trust what the preacher told me and assumed it was true. There wasn't any assurance in my heart or understanding of my own. I just followed their example and did what I was told. Then I received the Holy Spirit, and the One who had written the Bible started explaining it to me. He began revealing things to my heart. Instead of receiving information from the outside in, God Himself was teaching me from the inside out! John 14:26

describes this, **"But the Comforter, which is the Holy Ghost, whom the Father will send in my name, he shall teach you all things, and bring all things to your remembrance, whatsoever I have said unto you."** The difference was daylight and darkness!

In addition to revelation knowledge, I became bold and passionate for the Lord. God's awesome love and glorious presence constantly overwhelmed me. Witnessing converted from a religious chore into a daily delight. The sick received healing when I prayed for them. However, these wonderful things combined to create some problems as well. For instance, my newfound zeal also got me kicked out of my church!

Religious Prejudice Overcome

Everything indicated that I had been baptized in the Holy Spirit, except I didn't speak in tongues. Why? I'd been taught against it! The church I was raised in didn't believe in the baptism in the Holy Spirit and thought that tongues were of the devil. Ignorance and wrong teaching predisposed me against this gift. Although speaking in tongues was available, negative feelings and fear prevented me from using it.

It took me a long time to renew my mind to what God's Word said about my new relationship with the Holy Spirit. Two and a half years after receiving the baptism, I discovered that speaking in tongues was a valid gift from God for today. Then another six months passed before I understood enough to yield to the Holy Spirit and actually speak in tongues. Until I saw what God's Word said about this, my faith wasn't strong enough to walk in it (Rom. 10:17).

If it weren't for my religious prejudice, I could have spoken in tongues as soon as I was baptized in the Holy Spirit. However, those thoughts kept me from enjoying God's gift, because their root was unbelief. Until I overcame them and brought myself to the point of voluntarily stepping out in faith, I couldn't speak in tongues. But as soon as I did, my life changed just as dramatically as when I first received the Holy Spirit!

You don't have to speak in tongues; you get to! Besides, there's really no good reason not to! Speaking in tongues releases God's power in your life, and it's available to every Christian who has received the baptism in the Holy Spirit. If you're not speaking in tongues, you're missing out!

Chapter 6

Proof for Today

God's Word clearly teaches that the gift of tongues is for today. This can best be seen in the three chapters of the Bible that deal specifically with the gifts of the Holy Spirit—1 Corinthians 12, 13, and 14. In addition to speaking in tongues, the other gifts are the word of wisdom, the word of knowledge, faith, gifts of healing, working of miracles, prophecy, discerning of spirits, and interpretation of tongues (1 Cor. 12:8-10). *Although an exciting study in itself, further explanation of each individual gift is beyond the scope of our present purpose.*

The local body at Corinth was one of the most carnal churches in the entire New Testament. A man had committed incest with his father's wife (1 Cor. 5:1). Believers were suing each other (6:1, 6-7). They divided themselves according to their favorite Bible teacher (3:3-5). Gluttony and drunkenness characterized the Lord's Supper (11:20-22). Tongues were being given in church services without interpretation (14:26-28). Paul rebuked and corrected the Corinthians for all of this immaturity and sin.

These believers were carnal in spite of the gifts of the Spirit—not because of them! It's wrong to assume that the gifts are bad for you just because the Corinthians had so many problems. Actually, the opposite is true! Although maturity isn't instantly granted, the gifts of the Holy Spirit do promote spiritual growth. This is why three different times Paul advised this carnal, sinful bunch to earnestly **"desire spiritual gifts"** (1 Cor. 12:31, **14:1,** 14:39). He knew the gifts would help them mature. That's good proof you should be speaking in tongues!

Whom Do You Believe?

I started talking about the Lord once to a woman whose house I was painting. When she asked me why I'd left the Baptist church, I told her that they kicked me out after I received the baptism in the Holy Spirit.

"Are you talking about speaking in tongues?" she inquired.

"Yes, that's part of it. I do speak in tongues, and that's why they asked me to leave the church."

She thought for a moment, then politely added, "Well, my church would have kicked you out too."

I asked "Why would they do that?" and showed her 1 Corinthians 14:39. "The Bible clearly says here **'Forbid not to speak with tongues.'**" I've never forgotten her candid reply.

"Well, there are lots of things in the Bible our church doesn't believe."

With that, I knew I couldn't minister to her anymore, because God's Word was not the final authority in her Christian life. She, like so many others, had chosen to believe her denomination's doctrines above God's Word. This is why 1 Corinthians 13 remains the most misunderstood passage of Scripture regarding the gifts of the Holy Spirit today!

Better with Love

The gifts of the Holy Spirit are meant to be operated in love. This explains why Paul wrote, **"But covet earnestly the best gifts: and yet shew I unto you a more excellent way"** (1 Cor. 12:31), as he launched into his famous love passage (1 Cor. 13). Some people have tried to say that love is the *more excellent way.* However, the context clearly shows that all of Paul's comments concerning love in chapter 13 pertain specifically to the use of the gifts of the Holy Spirit listed in chapter 12 and expounded on immediately following in chapter 14. His point is not that love is better than the gifts but rather that operating the gifts in love is better than using them without it.

The Holy Spirit doesn't control you like a puppet! He leads, guides, and inspires you to speak in tongues and operate the other gifts, but you are the one who actually does it. Therefore, it's possible to operate in the gifts carnally, make mistakes, and fail to be motivated by love. **"Though I speak with the tongues of men and of angels, and have not charity, I am become as sounding brass, or a tinkling cymbal. And though I have the gift of prophecy, and understand all mysteries, and all knowledge; and though I have all faith, so that I could remove mountains, and have not charity, I am nothing"** (1 Cor. 13:1-2). It doesn't matter which gift you're operating in—tongues, prophecy, faith—there's no benefit apart from the right motive. Therefore, let love motivate your use of every gift of the Spirit—including speaking in tongues!

In fact, God's love should be the motivation for everything you do. **"And though I bestow all my goods to feed the poor, and though I give my body to be burned, and have not charity, it profiteth me nothing"** (1 Cor. 13:3). Whether you attend church because you feel you have to or give into an offering out of sheer obligation, apart from love, it profits you nothing. From God's point of view, your motive is more important than your action.

Until That Which Is Perfect Is Come

People who reject the baptism in the Holy Spirit twist 1 Corinthians 13:8-10 in order to support their position that tongues passed away with the early church. **"Charity never faileth: but whether there be prophecies, they shall fail; whether there be tongues, they shall cease; whether there be knowledge, it shall vanish away. For we know in part, and we prophesy in part. But when that which is perfect is come, then that which is in part shall be done away"** (1 Cor. 13:8-10). They claim that God only gave the gifts of the Holy Spirit (speaking in tongues, prophecy, gifts of healing, working of miracles, etc.) to the early church because the Bible wasn't written yet. Asserting that the Bible is "that which is perfect," they justify their conclusion that God doesn't do these things anymore. Nonsense!

If you read that passage in its context, you can easily see what it's really saying. Remember, Paul's subject for this entire section of Scripture (1 Cor. 12, 13, and 14) is properly operating the gifts of the Holy Spirit. He just finished saying that the gifts should be used in love (13:1-3). Verses 4-7 describe what that looks like. Then in verse 8, the Word states that when tongues cease, knowledge will too. Living in what's been popularly called "The Information Age," you and I both know that this hasn't happened yet. In fact, God's Word prophesies that in the end times knowledge will greatly increase (Dan. 12:4).

"For we know in part, and we prophesy in part. But <u>when that which is perfect is come</u>, then that which is in part shall be done away. When I was a child, I spake as a child, I understood as a child, I thought as a child: but when I became a man, I put away childish things. For now we see through a glass, darkly; but <u>then</u> face to face: now I know in part; but <u>then</u> shall I know even as also I am known" (1 Cor. 13:9-12, emphasis added). "Then" verse 12 refers to "when that which is perfect is come." At the time when that which is perfect is come, you will see Jesus face to face. Since that won't happen until the Lord's Second Coming or you die and go to be with Him, neither has tongues yet passed away.

"That which is perfect" refers to your glorified body, not the Bible. Yes, the Bible is perfect—inspired, inerrant, infallible—but it's not what this phrase is pointing to. When you receive your glorified body, you will no longer see through a glass darkly or know in part. In your glorified body, you will see Jesus face to face and know Him even as He knows you—completely. For now, speaking in tongues has been given to help you grow in the knowledge of Him. In your glorified body, you won't need tongues or the other gifts of the Holy Spirit—prophecy, the word of wisdom, discerning of spirits, interpretation of tongues, etc.—to reveal the Lord anymore, because you'll already know Him fully.

The very scriptures people use to dismiss the gifts of the Holy Spirit actually prove their validity for today! As long as your knowledge of Him is incomplete, the gifts of the Spirit will function. Until you see Jesus face to face in your glorified body, you need to be speaking in tongues. Since that which is perfect has yet to come, God's miraculous power continues on earth today just as it did for the early church. You would have to already be corrupted with a predisposed, religious mindset in order to honestly look at these scriptures and interpret them as saying, "God's miraculous power has passed away." **"Brethren, covet to prophesy, and forbid not to speak with tongues"** (1 Cor. 14:39)!

Miraculous Proof

Why do some people fight so hard against God's Word that the baptism of the Holy Spirit and His miraculous power is for today? Two main reasons are wrong teaching and a rejection of personal responsibility. Doctrines of men can render the Word of God ineffective. That's what happens when you hold on to religious tradition instead of God's Word (Mark 7:13). Also, there's a fear of having to produce biblical results. If you profess to believe in the baptism in the Holy Spirit, speaking in tongues, casting out demons, healing, and miracles, then that puts pressure on you to manifest them (Mark 16:17-18). Most people don't want to accept this kind of personal responsibility.

Instead, many hide behind a convenient theology. Calling themselves "Christian," they quickly confess that their sins are forgiven, while their lives offer very little proof. It's easy to profess, "My sins are forgiven," because you can't see a sin, and you can't see when it's forgiven. However, if miracles are really part of the Christian life, then there are things you can do to prove their reality. For instance, you can speak in tongues, cast a demon out, see blind eyes and deaf ears open, or even raise someone from the dead (I have personally done all of these things on multiple occasions and know many others who have done them as well—to God be the glory). In order to sit in front of the television living carnal, self-centered lives while defending their position of being forgiven, these people choose to believe only what God's Word says about forgiveness of sins while conveniently ignoring the rest. They may or may not truly be saved. Who would know?

Jesus used miracles to prove salvation. **"Whether is it easier to say to the sick of the palsy, Thy sins be forgiven thee; or to say, Arise, and take up thy bed, and walk? But that ye may know that the Son of man hath power on earth to forgive sins, (he saith to the sick of the palsy,) I say unto thee, Arise, and take up thy bed, and go thy way into thine house"** (Mark 2:9-11). Confronted by unbelieving, religious leaders, Jesus asked them which would be harder to say, "Your sins are forgiven" or "Take up your bed and walk." No one can see a sin forgiven, but everyone in that crowded room, including the Pharisees, would be able to see if this man was healed or not. Either he would get up and walk, or Jesus' words would be totally violated. Therefore, "Take up your bed and walk" was definitely harder to say!

The people knew if Jesus could perform that which was hardest, surely He could do the least. **"And immediately he arose, took up the bed, and went forth before them all; insomuch that they were all amazed, and glorified God"** (Mark 2:12). Jesus used this fact that He could heal bodies and perform miracles in the physical realm to substantiate the fact that He could also do things, like forgiving sins, in the spiritual realm.

Many people hide behind this false doctrine that miracles passed away so they can claim to be in relationship with God without ever doing anything that demonstrates it. That's just a convenient theology! The truth is that God still does miracles today, and you should be speaking in tongues until you receive your glorified body!

Chapter 7

Build Yourself Up

The primary purpose of speaking in tongues is to promote personal spiritual growth. **"For he that speaketh in an unknown tongue speaketh not unto men, but unto God: for no man understandeth him; howbeit in the spirit he speaketh mysteries...He that speaketh in an unknown tongue edifieth himself"** (1 Cor. 14:2, 4). When you speak in tongues, you're building yourself up spiritually.

You also keep yourself in the love of God. **"But ye, beloved, building up yourselves on your most holy faith, praying in the Holy Ghost, Keep yourselves in the love of God, looking for the mercy of our Lord Jesus Christ unto eternal life"** (Jude 1:20-21). God's love for you never changes, but your experience of it does. Speaking in tongues helps you fulfill your responsibility to keep yourself aware of and enjoying God's unfailing love.

Speaking in tongues produces rest and spiritual refreshment. **"For with stammering lips and another tongue will he speak to this people. To whom he said, This is the rest wherewith ye may cause the weary to rest; and this is the refreshing"** (Is. 28:11-12). Your spirit is the part of you where God lives. It's brand new, pure, righteous, and holy. When you pray in tongues, you release into your soul and body that rest and refreshment that's already in your spirit.

Personally, I encourage myself by speaking in tongues! Whenever I feel tired or discouraged, I pray in the spirit until rest and refreshment come. Despite negative circumstances and emotions, I'll exercise my faith to pray in tongues until I'm aware of and enjoying God's love again. Once you realize you can pray in the spirit any time you choose, you have no excuse to ever be depressed again!

Praying Perfectly

When you pray in tongues, your natural mind doesn't understand. **"For if I pray in an unknown tongue, my spirit prayeth, but my understanding is unfruitful"** (1 Cor. 14:14). Unless there's an interpretation, your intellect doesn't know what your spirit is praying.

Your spirit has the mind of Christ. **"For who hath known the mind of the Lord, that he may instruct him? But we have the mind of Christ"** (1 Cor. 2:16). Your spirit knows all things. **"But ye have an unction from the Holy One, and ye know all things"** (1 John 2:20). **"And have put on the new man, which is renewed in knowledge after the image of him that created him"** (Col. 3:10). Therefore, your spirit always knows how to pray perfectly for situations, yourself, and others.

There's a big difference between praying from your spirit and praying from your mind. Your natural mind typically has incomplete information. It lacks full knowledge of God's Word, the situation, and the people involved. Therefore, you cannot pray from your intellect with completeness and one hundred percent accuracy. However, since your born-again spirit knows all things, it's impossible to pray in tongues without praying God's will!

At times, the Holy Spirit may intercede for someone else through you as you pray in tongues. **"Likewise the Spirit also helpeth our infirmities: for we know not what we should pray for as we ought: but the Spirit itself maketh intercession for us with groanings which cannot be uttered. And he that searcheth the hearts knoweth what is the mind of the Spirit, because he maketh intercession for the saints according to the will of God"** (Rom. 8:26-27). This is especially helpful when your mind is not sure how to pray for a specific person or situation.

As you speak in tongues, you are speaking the hidden wisdom of God. Paul received the revelation for the messages he preached through speaking in tongues. **"Howbeit we speak wisdom among them that are perfect: yet not the wisdom of this world, nor of the princes of this world, that come to nought: But we speak the wisdom of God in a mystery, even the hidden wisdom, which God ordained before the world unto our glory"** (1 Cor. 2:6-7). **"For he that speaketh in an unknown tongue speaketh not unto men, but unto God: for no man understandeth him; howbeit in the spirit he speaketh mysteries"** (1 Cor. 14:2). As Paul spoke God's mysteries in tongues, he built himself up spiritually and revelation knowledge came. As you pray in tongues, you'll be built up spiritually as revelation knowledge comes to you too!

Chapter 8

Interpretation

When you speak in tongues, you should believe God for the interpretation. **"Wherefore let him that speaketh in an unknown tongue pray that he may interpret"** (1 Cor. 14:13). It's beyond your carnal ability to grasp the mysteries and hidden wisdom of God that you're praying in the spirit. However, if you ask Him, God will supernaturally give you the interpretation.

The public use of the gift of tongues in a church service requires interpretation. **"If any man speak in an unknown tongue, let it be by two, or at the most by three, and that by course; and let one interpret. But if there be no interpreter, let him keep silence in the church; and let him speak to himself, and to God"**

(1 Cor. 14:27-28). Without interpretation of a publicly given tongue, some people will think you're crazy. **"If therefore the whole church be come together into one place, and all speak with tongues, and there come in those that are unlearned, or unbelievers, will they not say that ye are mad"** (1 Cor. 14:23).

Certain members of the body are given the vocation of interpretation for public purposes. **"Now ye are the body of Christ, and members in particular. And God hath set some in the church, first apostles, secondarily prophets, thirdly teachers, after that miracles, then gifts of healings, helps, governments, diversities of tongues. Are all apostles? are all prophets? are all teachers? are all workers of miracles? Have all the gifts of healing? do all speak with tongues? do all interpret"** (1 Cor. 12:27-30).

Some people have misunderstood 1 Corinthians 12:29-30 to mean that not everyone should speak in tongues. However, Mark 16:17-18 states, **"And these signs shall follow them that believe; In my name shall they cast out devils; they shall speak with new tongues; They shall take up serpents; and if they drink any deadly thing, it shall not hurt them; they shall lay hands on the sick, and they shall recover."** Therefore, some have vocations of speaking and/or interpreting tongues given publicly in a church service, but every Spirit-baptized believer can pray in tongues for personal edification.

Of Men and Angels

Tongues come in two different types: tongues of men and tongues of angels. **"Though I speak with the tongues of men and of angels"** (1 Cor. 13:1).

Tongues of men are languages that either have been or are spoken on earth. When the disciples were first baptized in the Holy Spirit on Pentecost, they spoke in tongues of men (Acts 2:4-12). This wasn't merely a supernatural acceleration of language learning, because the speakers themselves had no idea what they were saying. The disciples didn't study all those different languages in the Upper Room while waiting for the promise! The Holy Spirit suddenly baptized them, and their tongues became a supernatural sign to the unbelievers within earshot whose native languages they spoke (1 Cor. 14:22).

Tongues of angels are heavenly languages. Every Spirit-baptized believer can pray in the tongues of angels. When you speak mysteries and the hidden wisdom of God, you are speaking in an angelic tongue.

It doesn't matter if you speak in a tongue of men or an angelic tongue, you can ask God for the interpretation!

Light in My Closet

Learning to believe God for interpretation turned my life around! When I first prayed in tongues after being baptized in the Holy Spirit, I remember hearing God speak to me in my heart as revelation knowledge began to flow. However, when I started sharing what God had shown me in His Word, people criticized and informed me I was wrong, because they had never heard these truths before. Feeling isolated and alone, I really struggled with what others were telling me and what I was hearing in my heart. In the midst of all this, I just kept seeking the Lord.

For six months, I meditated on God's Word all day long. I'd focus my attention on each individual word and phrase as I wrote out hundreds of scriptures by hand daily. After meditating this way for eight to ten hours, God's Word exploded with meaning in my heart, but my mind struggled to understand. So I'd shut myself in my closet to pray in the spirit for another hour or two. Sitting there underneath my clothes, I'd ask God to interpret to my natural understanding what I'd been studying. Then, I'd pray in tongues for the purpose of personal edification.

At the end of that season, my trickle of revelation knowledge suddenly burst forth into a mighty rushing river! In fact, I received so much so fast that I finally told God I couldn't handle any more. It was just more than I could retain! Much of what I'm teaching today—over thirty-five years later—came as a result of what I learned at that time. I simply prayed in tongues and believed to interpret!

Gain Understanding

All you need to interpret tongues for personal edification is to gain understanding. When you're praying by yourself, you don't have to stop and get an interpretation in English. This method—praying out loud in tongues, then waiting until the English interpretation is given—works well in public, but it's not the only way to receive interpretation. You just need your mind to become fruitful!

God encouraged me through an experience that happened while I was still quite new at this. Since I'd been taught against tongues so strongly, I still wrestled with doubts about whether all my praying in the spirit was really beneficial or not. After spending two hours speaking in tongues one morning, someone whom I hadn't seen in four years showed up at my house. He knocked on the door, rushed in without greeting me, plopped down on my couch, and burst into tears. My first thought was, *I should have been praying in English instead of wasting all morning praying in tongues!* Then it dawned on me, *How would I have known to pray for this guy unless I had been praying in tongues?* My spirit had been praying perfectly!

All of a sudden, faith rose up inside as I stopped him mid-sentence, interrupting his blubbering attempt to explain the situation. By revelation knowledge, I finished describing the rest of his problem—and nailed it! This supernatural demonstration of God's power and love totally set him free! Through this, the Lord confirmed to me that I'd been praying in tongues for this situation earlier, and all I had to do was interpret. What I spoke to this man was the interpretation!

Mind Your Head!

When you pray in tongues, your mind can be occupied with something else. Since your spirit's praying and not your brain, your mind can wander. You can even think about things totally unrelated to God! That's why some people like to read the Word, enjoy godly music, or listen to Bible teaching while they pray in tongues. Others pray in the spirit while working, driving, or doing household chores. Personally, I've trained myself to pray with my understanding while praying in tongues.

When I'd pray in the spirit over longer periods of time, people whom I hadn't thought of in years would come to mind. At first, I just dismissed it, but when they'd suddenly call, send a letter, or even show up at my house—like that fellow did—I began realizing that God was giving me interpretations. They weren't always word for word but also came as impressions, pictures, and unctions. As I recognized the Lord bringing these people to mind, I'd start praying for them. Then, I'd follow through and see miracles happen every time!

God led me to call a good friend of mine one time after praying in tongues. We'd been out of touch with each other for several years. He answered the phone and immediately hung up on me. His reaction seemed strange since I knew God had prompted me to call. While sitting at my desk pondering this, the phone rang. Sure enough, it was my friend! He explained that he had just told God how he had spent his entire life ministering to others, but now that he was in need, nobody was ministering to him. My friend had barely finished praying "God, please send somebody to encourage me, or I'm going to quit the ministry!" when the phone rang and there I was. He was so startled, he hung up the receiver! This whole incident resulted from interpreting a tongue.

You can do this while praying for people, when you need wisdom for a challenging situation, or simply to understand a particular scripture. Just take the person, situation, or passage, and begin praying in tongues over it. As you're praying, ask the Lord to show you what it means. Although understanding may not always come at that exact moment, God will give you an interpretation.

My friend prays in tongues over church services he's going to minister in. He prefers to receive the interpretation right away so he'll know in advance what God wants to do, who's going to be healed of what, etc. Personally, I don't always like to receive the interpretation right away. If God supernaturally told me what was going to happen at a church service a week away, my mind would try to analyze the situation and figure it all out in the meantime. I pray in tongues often without receiving anything from the Lord at that moment. However, when I need it a week or a month later, I'll ask God for the interpretation of what I've been praying in tongues about. At that point, I receive exactly what I need from the Holy Spirit!

As you step out in faith to pray in tongues and believe God for the interpretation, you'll receive exactly what you need from the Holy Spirit too!

Chapter 9

Get Started

Speaking in tongues is not something you do just once to prove you've received the baptism in the Holy Spirit. It's a powerful tool to edify yourself spiritually. Whenever you pray in tongues, you cause yourself to rest, you build yourself up on your most holy faith, and you keep the love of God active and alive in your heart. As you speak forth hidden wisdom and believe for interpretation, revelation knowledge will open up and supply answers you couldn't get any other way. That's why the devil has fought so hard against this gift! He's afraid of what would happen if speaking in tongues ever became part of your daily Christian life.

The Holy Spirit inspires the words, but you have to say them. **"And they were all filled with the Holy Ghost, and began to speak with other tongues, as**

the Spirit gave them utterance" (Acts 2:4). Notice that the Spirit gave <u>them</u> utterance. It's not just purely the Holy Spirit speaking through you. He gives you a prodding and a desire, but you must do the talking.

It's similar to how the gift of teaching works. If I stood before a group of people and prayed "God, please speak through me, but don't let me say anything that's not of You" and then waited for Him to make me speak, I'd never say anything. It's my responsibility to step out in faith and start talking. God inspires the messages, but they come out through my personality, vocabulary, and mannerisms. God doesn't speak in Texas drawl; I do! The Holy Spirit supplies the content and I deliver it!

Fear short-circuits your ability to speak in tongues. You might have trouble at first if you worry about it or try to analyze what you're saying. The problem isn't with the Holy Spirit not inspiring, but rather it's with your fear that's blocking it. Yield your tongue to the Holy Spirit, and then speak forth by faith the words that He gives you.

Breakthrough!

I struggled to pray in tongues for months. Even though I was convinced it was of God and wanted it, I had a hard time receiving my prayer language.

A man came over to my house in an attempt to help

me. He asked, "If you repeated something I said in Spanish, would you be speaking in Spanish?" I nodded. "Then if I spoke something in tongues and you repeated it, would you be speaking in tongues?"

"Yes, but I don't want to just repeat something. I want to speak in tongues on my own!" He kept insisting, so finally I gave in. However, I stopped after only getting through the first couple of words. Embarrassed, I told him I wasn't doing a very good job repeating what he said.

He argued, "Yeah, but you were speaking in tongues. That wasn't English!"

By then I had reached my limit. "No, I don't accept that. I wasn't speaking in tongues!" He just threw up his hands in frustration and left.

Immediately after this, I was on my way to minister to someone. In desperation I declared, "God, I'm just going to start talking. I believe that You are going to help me speak in tongues." Then I began making up nonsense words and saying them out loud. It seemed silly to me, so I didn't feel very good about it. However, I realized that I'd said two words that did sound pretty decent. Since they seemed like a real language to me, I figured they must be tongues. So I took those two words and started speaking them over and over again all the way to my destination.

Upon arrival, I experienced the best time of ministry I'd ever had before. I was convinced it was because I'd been praying in tongues. On my way home, I started praising God in the car and decided to pray using those two words some more, but I panicked when I couldn't remember them. After struggling so long to pray in tongues, I had forgotten the only two words I'd received!

Then I thought, *I'll just get another two!* So I started the process over again until another two words came. After using them for a while, I added a couple more. Within a few moments, I was speaking fluently in tongues!

Looking back, I know now that I could have spoken in tongues all along. However, I was under the false impression that the Holy Spirit would come upon me with such force that I wouldn't be able to keep myself from blurting out in tongues. When that never happened, I discovered He doesn't work that way. The Holy Spirit was just waiting for me to speak out in faith the words He'd been gently inspiring me to say.

Now it's your turn to do the same!

Let's Pray

Father, thank You for baptizing me in the Holy Spirit! I'm so grateful You gave me this wonderful gift. Please help me to walk in all of its benefits!

Through speaking in tongues, I can draw on the power You've placed within me: for rest and refreshing, for building my faith and keeping myself in Your love, and for revelation knowledge as interpretation comes.

I am a believer! **Your Word says, "These signs shall follow them that believe; In my name shall they cast out devils; they shall speak with new tongues"** (Mark 16:17). *By faith, I will speak in tongues from this day forward, in Jesus' name. Amen!*

Father Is Proud of You!

Now, by faith, say out loud those sounds coming up from deep within. You'll be talking in a language unknown to you, but the Holy Spirit is the One inspiring it. You'll be speaking in tongues!

Go ahead—practice awhile! Enjoy yourself in the Lord!

If you aren't fluent right away, don't worry—God is proud of you! When little children start to speak, their parents know what they are trying to say. Even though it's baby talk, they're pleased. Your heavenly Father is proud of you, even if your tongue isn't fluent yet. If you'll just keep using it and not worry about yourself so much, tongues will begin to flow out of you unhindered!

As your brother in the Lord, I welcome you to the Spirit-filled life!

Receiving Jesus as your Savior

Choosing to receive Jesus Christ as your Lord and Savior is the most important decision you'll ever make!

God's Word promises **"that if thou shalt confess with thy mouth the Lord Jesus, and shalt believe in thine heart that God hath raised him from the dead, thou shalt be saved. For with the heart man believeth unto righteousness; and with the mouth confession is made unto salvation"** (Rom. 10:9-10). **"For whosoever shall call upon the name of the Lord shall be saved"** (Rom. 10:13).

By His grace, God has already done everything to provide salvation. Your part is simply to believe and receive.

Pray out loud, *"Jesus, I confess that You are my Lord and Savior. I believe in my heart that God raised You from the dead. By faith in Your Word, I receive salvation now. Thank You for saving me!"*

The very moment you commit your life to Jesus Christ, the truth of His Word instantly comes to pass in your spirit. Now that you're born again, there's a brand-new you!

Receiving the Holy Spirit

As His child, your loving heavenly Father wants to give you the supernatural power you need to live this new life.

"For every one that asketh receiveth; and he that seeketh findeth; and to him that knocketh it shall be opened...how much more shall your heavenly Father give the Holy Spirit to them that ask him?" (Luke 11:10,13).

All you have to do is ask, believe, and receive!

Pray, *"Father, I recognize my need for Your power to live this new life. Please fill me with Your Holy Spirit. By faith, I receive it right now! Thank You for baptizing me! Holy Spirit, You are welcome in my life!"*

Congratulations—now you're filled with God's supernatural power!

Some syllables from a language you don't recognize will rise up from your heart to your mouth (1 Cor 14:14). As you speak them out loud by faith, you're releasing God's power from within and building yourself up in the spirit (1 Cor14:4). You can do this whenever and wherever you like!

It doesn't really matter whether you felt anything or not when you prayed to receive the Lord and His Spirit. If you believed in your heart that you received, then God's Word promises you did. **"Therefore I say unto you, What things soever ye desire, when ye pray, believe that ye receive them, and ye shall have them"** (Mark 11:24). God always honors His Word. Believe it!

Please contact me and let me know that you've prayed to receive Jesus as your Savior or be filled with the Holy Spirit. I would like to rejoice with you and help you understand more fully what has taken place in your life. I'll send you a free gift that will help you understand and grow in your new relationship with the Lord. *"Welcome to your new life!"*

Recommended Materials

Spirit, Soul & Body

Understanding the relationship of your spirit, soul, and body is foundational to your Christian life. You will never truly know how much God loves you or believe what His Word says about you until you do. Learn how they're related and how that knowledge will release the life of your spirit into your body and soul. It may even explain why many things are not working the way you had hoped.

Item Code: 1027   4-Tape album
Item Code: 1027-C   4-CD album

Eternal Life

Is eternal life just about living forever, or could there be more? What does God's Word say? Andrew's answer to this question may change the way you view salvation and your approach to your relationship with God. This single teaching is the first from the *Introducing Discipleship Evangelism* album.

Item Code: DE01   Single Tape
Item Code: DE01-C   Single CD

Water Baptism

What is water baptism all about? What really happens when you get baptized? How should it be done? These are just a few of the question Don Krow will answer from the Word of God concerning baptism.

Item Code: 67K   Single Tape

A Sure Foundation

God's Word is the only true foundation for your life. Listen as Andrew explains the supernatural process that occurs when you plant the Word in your heart. He uses the example of how Jesus dealt with John the Baptist's unbelief to reveal the power of the Word.

Item Code: 1034   4-Tape album

Introducing Discipleship Evangelism

Did God call us to make converts or disciples? It's an important question. The misunderstanding of that has led to some appalling statistics. Many evangelists now realize that only about 15 percent of those who accept Jesus continue in the faith. It's time we changed our thinking and started practicing what Jesus taught. Learn more in this enlightening series.

Item Code: 1028   3-Tape album
Item Code: 1028-C   3-CD album

Contact Information

Andrew Wommack Ministries, Inc.
P.O. Box 3333
Colorado Springs, CO 80934
Helpline Phone 719-635-1111
www.awmi.net

Andrew Wommack Ministries of Europe
P.O. Box 4392
Walsall WS1 9AR
England
Helpline Phone +44 (0) 1922 473 300
www.awme.net

About the Author

Andrew Wommack

For over three decades Andrew has traveled America and the world teaching the truth of the Gospel. His profound revelation of the Word of God is taught with clarity and simplicity, emphasizing God's unconditional love and the balance between grace and faith. He reaches millions of people through the daily *Gospel Truth* radio and television programs, broadcast both domestically and internationally. He founded Charis Bible College in 1994 and has since established CBC extension colleges in other major cities of America and around the world. Andrew has produced a library of teaching materials, available in print, audio, and visual formats. And, as it has been from the beginning, his ministry continues to distribute free audio tapes and CDs to those who cannot afford them.